I Can Have What I Say

Book Series

Everyday Prayers for Young Adults

L. Toy Pridegon

WHAT YOU SAY PUBLISHING Flint, Mich.

I Can Have What I Say Book Series

Everyday Prayers for Young Adults

© 2023 L. Toy Pridegon

Published by WHAT YOU SAY PUBLISHING

Flint, Michigan 48504

ISBN: 979-8-9881437-1-0

Printed in the United States 10 9 8 7 6 5 4 3 2 1

For Worldwide Distribution

All Scriptures used came from:

- Amplified Bible (AMP)

- Amplified Bible, Classic Edition (APMC)

- King James (KJV)

- New Living Translation (NLT)

- The Message Bible (MSG)

- Evangelical Heritage Version (EHV)

- English Standard Version (ESV)

- The Living Bible (TLB)

- The Voice (Voice)

DEDICATION

The prayers written in this book have been written so you can experience and maintain success in every area of your life.

God wants you to know Him intimately, He wants you to know that you can and should come to Him in good times and bad, whether or not you've walked in obedience to Him or messed up big time. He wants you to always come boldly to the Throne of Grace in prayer. He wants you to come and pray to the Father in Jesus Name.

PREFACE

Each book in the "I Can Have What I Say" series is to be used as a tool to: teach the prayer warrior how to pray accurately and with specificity; build confidence; increase your faith; help you to patiently endure as you wait for the manifestation of your prayers that by faith have already been answered.

ACKNOWLEDGMENTS

I would, of course, like to thank God for leading me and giving me the strength to write this book, my second book in the series of: I Can Have What I Say books. My life is on display in the pages of every book I write.

Second, I would like to thank my family, who through the many circumstances we've faced, brought me to my knees in prayer and taught me how to wait patiently for the manifestation of what was speaking into existence.

Last but certainly not least I would like to thank my husband whose unconditional love, support, patience, discernment and prayers keep me grounded, focused and able to accomplish much in the kingdom of Go

CONTENTS

EVERYDAY PRAYERS FOR YOUNG ADULTS

EVERYDAY PRAYERS FOR YOUNG ADULTS

INTRODUCTION

Prayer is saying things that haven't happened yet, a speaking those things that are not real yet as if they were real right now. Your mind won't want you to say such things because it almost feels like you're lying, but NO! You are speaking words filled with faith. You are behaving like God wants you to, speaking His language. Now you are walking by faith and not by sight. Soon your heart will believe the words your mouth speaks and your ears hear. He hears you and rest assured He is going to make sure your prayer, which is according to His will for you, shall come to pass.

Romans 4:17-18 The Message (MSG) Speak those things that be not as though as they were

[17-18] We call Abraham "father" not because he got God's attention by living like a saint, but because God made something out of Abraham when he was a nobody. Isn't that what we've always read in Scripture, God saying to Abraham, "I set you up as father of many peoples"? Abraham was first named "father" and then *became* a father because he dared

to trust God to do what only God could do: raise the dead to life, with a word make something out of nothing. When everything was

11

hopeless, Abraham believed anyway, deciding to live not on the basis of what he saw he *couldn't* do but on

what God said he *would* do. And so he was made father of a multitude of peoples. God himself said to him, "You're going to have a big family, Abraham!"

Mark 11:23-24 Amplified Bible (AMP) Believe that you receive

[23] I assure you *and* most solemnly say to you, whoever says to this mountain, 'Be lifted up and thrown into the sea!' and does not doubt in his heart [in God's unlimited power], but believes that what he says is going to take place, it will be done for him [in accordance with God's will]. [24] For this reason I am telling you, whatever things you ask for in prayer [in accordance with God's will], believe [with confident trust] that you have received them, and they will be *given* to you.

2 Corinthians 5:7 Amplified Bible (AMP) Act like it's already done

[7] for we walk by faith, not by sight [living our lives in a manner consistent with our confident belief in God's promises]

HOW TO USE EVERYDAY PRAYER FOR YOUNG ADULTS

1. Simply pray or read the prayers aloud that are relevant to your life or the lives of others.
2. End each prayer in Jesus Name.
3. Read the scripture reference.
4. Pray until what you're believing for manifests

WHAT IS PRAYER

Prayer is asking God to do something for you, or on behalf of someone else. It involves speaking and even more importantly, listening. You are speaking faith filled words, speaking as if you already have what you are asking for. This is what's called "speaking those things that be not as though they were" according to Romans 8:4-17. If you're not used to praying this way it may seem strange at first; some people refuse to pray this way because they feel as if they are lying, but no, you're not lying. This is how you walk by faith by speaking Gods Word, which can be contrary to your situation.

WHEN SHOULD YOU PRAY

You should pray every chance you get, I Thessalonians 5:17, KJV says: Pray without ceasing. The Amplified Bible says: Be unceasing and persistent in prayer. I would suggest that you pick a specific time of day to pray, developing a lifestyle of prayer, so it becomes a part of your daily routine. However, any time and every opportunity is a good time to pray, location permitting

WHERE SHOULD YOU PRAY

You can pray anywhere. In the shower, in your room, on your break at work, at school between classes. No place is off limits unless prayer is not allowed or you would be disruptive or out of order to do so.

HOW LONG SHOULD YOU PRAY

Jesus asked the disciples to pray (Matthew 26:36-40) and rebuked or chastised them when they didn't. Now while this is a good standard to live up to because we are followers of Christ, the most important thing is that you

are faithful to pray at least once every day then how long you pray will take care of itself.

WHY SHOULD YOU PRAY

You should pray because we communicate with God this way. You should pray because in life you will be faced with many obstacles, dilemmas and circumstances that God can and will help you with but you must ask in faith through prayer.

WHAT SHOULD YOU PRAY FOR

You can and should pray for whatever concerns you at any given time. Nothing that will ever happen to you, for you or because of you, is a surprise to God. So take everything to God in prayer, He wants you to.

TYPES OF PRAYER

1. PRAYER OF THANKSGIVING

The Prayer of Thanksgiving is thanking God for what He has done (Colossians 4:2). It is a good practice to either begin and or end your prayers by giving thanks.

2. PRAYER OF SUPPLICATION

The prayer of supplication is when you pray, you can ask God for something for yourself and give Him thanks for it. Philippians 4:6 says ...by prayer and supplication

with thanksgiving you can ask God to do something for you.

3. INTERCESSORY PRAYER

Intercessory prayer is praying on behalf of others as Abraham did for Sodom and Gomorrah in Genesis 18:23-34.

4. WORSHIP

The prayer of Worship is thanking God for who He is. It is a good practice to either begin and or end your prayers, in addition to giving thanks, with worship (Psalm 95:2-3).

5. PRAYER OF CONSECRATION

The prayer of consecration is praying to know Gods will (Luke 26:39), Jesus prayed to be assured of Gods will.

6. PRAYER OF IMPORTUNITY

The Prayer of Importunity is a prayer of persistence, to insist on having, will not give up, a relentless, consistent petition. (Luke 11:9)

7. PRAYER OF FAITH OR FAITH FILLED PRAYERS

The Prayer of Faith will heal the sick (James 5:15).

If you expect to receive an answer to your prayers, then your prayers must be filled with words of faith according to Mark 11:22-25. Faith Filled Prayers consist of:

- Praying according to God's Word
- Believing the prayer you prayed
- Receive the answer before you see the answer by giving God praise
- Act like it's already done

Each prayer in this book contains one or a combination of these prayers. As you become more familiar with prayer and the types of prayer, you'll know which type of prayer you are praying at any given time.

PROLOGUE

From my heart to yours

You have to know, never forget and always remember, that you are EXCEPTIONAL, EXTRAORDINARY, VALUABLE, WORTHY, LOVED, WONDERFULLY MADE, FAVORED, MORE THAN A CONQUEROR, A WINNER, A CHAMPION AND YOU DESERVE THE VERY BEST.

How do I know this about you? Because God created you that's how I know. God never creates junk or anything ugly or unusable. God NEVER makes mistakes. When God created you, He was having a great day. He took His time and thought about exactly how He wanted you to look and what He wanted you to do and be in life. In other words, God has a Purpose, a plan for your life, a destiny to fulfill. The only thing about your purpose is you will have to discover it. Once you discover your purpose, there will be obstacles in the way to the fulfillment of it. So, you must pray. You are not

excused from prayer or doing the will of God because of your age. I advise you to search out more scriptures on each topic, read, study and memorize some of them.

The prayers in this book will help you overcome whatever you may be faced with; give you wisdom on how to handle situations; give you peace when things seem chaotic; strength when you feel like you can't make it and remind you that all things work out for your good. You've already won, God said so! Just pray.

Jesus loves you and so do I!

LET'S PRAY

PRAYER OF PRAISE AND THANKSGIVING

Father,

I give You thanks and praise today for all the great things You've done for me. I thank You for waking me up today and watching over me as I slept. I thank You for always making a way for me and setting my life on a path of total victory. I thank You for providing for my every need and even granting my Godly heart's desires. Lord, I thank You for loading me up with the benefits of Peace, unconditional Love, Joy and Righteousness. I thank You for Your mercy which never comes to an end but is new every morning.

In Jesus Name! Amen

SCRIPTURE REFERENCE:

Hebrews 13:15 Amplified Bible (AMP)

Through Him, therefore, let us at all times offer up to God a sacrifice of praise, which is the fruit of lips that thankfully acknowledge and confess and glorify His name.

PRAYER OF WORSHIP

Father,

I come to worship You for who You are. I love You, Lord, and magnify Your Name. I appreciate and honor You, Lord. I bless You and give glory to your Name. You are the King of kings and the Lord of lords, the Beginning and the End and I worship You. I magnify You and lift up your Name. I see you high and lifted up and Your train fills the temple. You are my Peace, my Healer, and Deliverer and I worship You. Lord, you are my Provider, my Victory, You are the Most High God, Lord you are worthy of all honor, glory and power. I'll have no other gods before You. You and You only will I worship, honor, adore and serve.
In Jesus Name! Amen.

SCRIPTURE REFERENCE:

Psalm 95:6 King James Version (KJV)
O come, let us worship and bow down: let us kneel before the Lord our maker.

CLOSER WALK WITH GOD

Father,

I want to be, I need to be closer to You. So, I thank You for a closer walk with You. I thank You for the desire to pray more, to read and study the bible more, to worship and praise more. I thank You that as I give You more of me, I'll have more of You. More of Your Peace, Wisdom, Joy, more of everything that You are. Your Word says that as I come close to You, You'll come close to me.

In Jesus Name! Amen.

SCRIPTURE REFERENCE

James 4:8 Amplified Bible (AMP)
[8] Come close to God [with a contrite heart] and He will come close to you. Wash your hands, you sinners; and purify your [unfaithful] hearts, you double-minded [people].

TO KNOW GOD'S WILL

Father,

I thank You that Your Word says I am a wonderful creation and You have made plans for my life. You knew me before I was born. Your plans for me are good and not evil, to give hope for an amazing future in You. So, I ask You now to reveal Your purpose and those plans for me, now in this season of my life and I thank You for it.

In Jesus Name! Amen.

SCRIPTURE REFERENCE:

Jeremiah 29:11 Amplified Bible (AMP)

[11] For I know the plans *and* thoughts that I have for you,' says the LORD, 'plans for peace *and* well-being and not for disaster, to give you a future and a hope.

HEALTHY SELF - ESTEEM

Father,

I thank you for creating me perfect in every way. I am the apple of your eye, Your special treasure. I am good looking, highly favored, accepted and loved unconditionally by You. Therefore I love and accept myself the way you created me. I see myself as a vessel of honor, fit for Your use, whole and complete in every way. There is nothing missing or broken in me. I will think highly of myself but not more highly than I should.

In Jesus name! Amen.

SCRIPTURE REFERENCE

Psalm 139:14 Amplified Bible (AMP)
[14] I will give thanks *and* praise to You, for I am fearfully and wonderfully made;
Wonderful are Your works,
And my soul knows it very well.

INTEGRITY – CHARACTER - HONESTY

Father,

I thank you for creating me in Your image, after Your likeness from the inside out. Because I am like You, I can keep and honor my word because You keep and honor Your Word. Because you are honest and truthful, I can be honest and truthful too. Because your character is good I will be a person of good character as well. I can do all things because You are in me and give me strength.

In Jesus Name! Amen.

SCRIPTURE REFERENCE

2 Corinthians 8:21 Amplified Bible (AMP)

[21] For we have regard for what is honorable [and above suspicion], not only in the sight of the Lord, but also in the sight of men.

TO BE A GOOD FRIEND

Father,

I thank you for showing me how to be a true, Godly friend and surrounding me with the same. I will be loyal, trustworthy and supportive. I thank you for friends who I can walk together with in true unity and unconditional love. I'll have their back and they'll have mine. I thank you for friends that love you like I do. Above all Lord I thank You for being the Friend that sticks closer than a brother who is always with me.

In Jesus Name! Amen.

SCRIPTURE REFERENCE

Proverbs 18:24 King James Version (KJV)
[24] A man that hath friends must shew himself friendly: and there is a friend that sticketh closer than a brother.

FOCUS

Father,

I thank You for showing me my purpose for this time in my life. The Purpose that gives my life vision. This vision is what I will focus on and pay attention to, set my priorities according to, receive strength from, order my life according to and pursue with all my heart. In Jesus Name!

WRITE YOUR VISION DOWN' THE THINGS YOU WANT TO DO. Even if you're not sure about it. God will correct or affirm what you write. Trust Him.

SCRIPTURE REFERENCE:

Habakkuk 2:2 Amplified Bible (AMP)

2 Then the LORD answered me and said, "Write the vision and engrave it plainly on [clay] tablets
So that the one who reads it will run.

WISDOM and GUIDANCE

Father, you said that I can ask You for wisdom when I need it. So, I ask and thank You for the wisdom and guidance to know what to do (**Speak the situation).** You know my comings and goings, You give my life direction. Lord, I thank You for the leading of Your Spirit to help me make the right choice according to Your purpose and plan for me.

In Jesus Name! Amen.

SCRIPTURE REFERENCE:

James 1:5 Amplified Bible (AMP)
[5] If any of you lacks wisdom [to guide him through a decision or circumstance], he is to ask of [our benevolent] God, who gives to everyone generously and without rebuke *or* blame, and it will be given to him.

MY PARENT(S)

Father,

I thank you for a good relationship with my parent(s). I thank you that according to Your Wisdom and perfect plan, You selected them to parent me. I thank you for their support, wisdom, and love. I thank you Lord for watching over them and keeping them safe and satisfying them with a long life, for keeping them healthy and strong, I thank You for keeping their bodies healed and their minds whole. And thank You form giving me favor with them.

In Jesus Name! Amen.

SCRIPTURE REFERENCE

Ephesians 6:1-3 Voice (THE VOICE)

Now to you, children, obey your parents in the Lord because this is right *in God's eyes.* [2] This is the first commandment onto which He added a promise: "Honor your father and your mother, and [3] if you do, you will live long and well in this land."[a]

TO OBEY MY PARENTS

Father,

I thank You for my parents, I thank You for hand selecting them to shape me into who You want me to be and everything You do is very good. I thank You that Your Word says I am to obey them. Even when I don't understand them, Lord I choose Your will and not my own, I choose to do what is right. With Your help, I will obey my parents.

In Jesus Name! Amen.

SCRIPTURE REFERENCE:

Ephesians 6:1 Amplified Bible (AMP)
6 Children, you belong to the Lord, and you do the right thing when you obey your parents. The first commandment with a promise says, [2] "Obey your father and your mother, [3] and you will have a long and happy life."

TO HONOR MY PARENTS

Father,

I thank You for my parents, no matter what, I choose to honor and respect them because Your Word says I should. Even though I don't always agree or understand, I choose to believe they always try to do their best. I thank You for all that they are and are not. I thank You for choosing them to help me be all that I am and shall be. I will honor my parents.

In Jesus Name! Amen.

SCRIPTURE REFERENCE:

Ephesians 6:2-3 Amplified Bible (AMP)
[2] HONOR [esteem, value as precious] YOUR FATHER AND YOUR MOTHER [and be respectful to them]—this is the first commandment with a promise— [3] SO THAT IT MAY BE WELL WITH YOU, AND THAT YOU MAY HAVE A LONG LIFE ON THE EARTH.

PRAYER FOR EVERYONE IN AUTHORITY

Father,

According to Your word, today, I pray for people who are in positions of authority so we can live in peace, safety and freedom. I pray for Kings, Presidents, State and City leaders, people in positions of Management and Administration, Entrepreneurs, Teachers and Police Officers. I pray that any of these individuals that don't know You, accept You today. I pray that they walk uprightly before You; seek out and surround themselves with Godly people to help them exercise good judgement and make wise decisions. Lord, help them do their jobs well and with integrity.

In Jesus Name! Amen.

SCRIPTURE REFERENCE:

1 Timothy 2:1-2 Amplified Bible (AMP)
1 First of all, then, I urge that petitions (specific requests), prayers, intercessions (prayers for others) and thanksgivings be offered on behalf of all people,
2 for [a]kings and all who are in [positions of] high authority, so that we may live a peaceful and quiet life in all godliness and dignity.

SUBMISSION TO AUTHORITY

Father,

Because Your Word says that I am to submit to authority, I will do just that. All authority, whether in school, at work, the government, at church, community Elders, everywhere. For as I submit to authority, I am submitting to You. Your Word is always right! I will submit to all authority as unto You.

In Jesus Name! Amen.

SCRIPTURE REFERENCE:

Romans 13:1 Amplified Bible (AMP)
13 Let every person be subject to the governing authorities. For there is no authority except from God [granted by His permission and sanction], and those which exist have been put in place by God.

DOING WELL ACADEMICALLY

Father,

 In Jesus Name I thank you that my life has a purpose. Part of that purpose is for me to go to school at every appointed time and get good grades and G.P.A. Therefore, I thank you for the desire to develop and practice good study habits so I can focus and be alert in class, set educational goals and keep them, and graduate on time. I thank you for placing in me everything I need to succeed.

In Jesus Name!

SCRIPTURE REFERENCE:

Philippians 4:13 Amplified Bible (AMP)
[13] I can do all things [which He has called me to do] through Him who strengthens *and* empowers me [to fulfill His purpose—I am self-sufficient in Christ's sufficiency; I am ready for anything and equal to anything through Him who infuses me with inner strength and confident peace.]

TAKING A TEST

Father,

I thank You that I am well able to meet any and every challenge set before me. I can do ALL things because You give me strength. I am prepared. Therefore, I thank You for helping me to remember everything I've learned. I am more than a conqueror and I have the mind of Christ, therefore I will pass this test and every test.

In Jesus Name! Amen.

Scripture Reference:

Romans 8:37 Amplified Bible (AMP)
[37] Yet in all these things we are more than conquerors *and* gain an overwhelming victory through Him who loved us [so much that He died for us].

BEING ORGANIZED - TIME MANAGEMENT

Father,

I thank you that time and opportunity happens for everyone, even me, and there is a time to do everything I need and want to do. Therefore I will make plans for each day and allow myself time to be on time. I will study when I need to study, work when I need to work and play when it's time to play. I can and will do all things, decently and in order. I thank you that you have ordered my steps so I will not make any missteps; I will use all my time wisely.

In Jesus Name! Amen

SCRIPTURE REFERENCE:

Ecclesiastes 3:1 Amplified Bible (AMP)
3 There is a season (a time appointed) for everything and a time for every delight *and* event *or* purpose under heaven—

TEACHERS – PROFESSORS - INSTRUCTORS

Father,

I thank you for the individuals that teach and instruct me. Father, give them the strength, wisdom, patience, creativity and enthusiasm to teach effectively so they would always have joy and passion as long as they teach. Lord watch over them in their comings and goings, meet their every need so they won't be stressed out. And Father I pray that any that don't know You would seek to know you that their joy may be full.

In Jesus Name! Amen.

SCRIPTURE REFERENCE:

Colossians 1:11 Amplified Bible (AMP)
[11] [we pray that you may be]
strengthened *and* invigorated with all power, according to His glorious might, to attain every kind of endurance and patience with joy;

FOR MY FELLOW CLASSMATES

Father,

I pray for my classmates today. I ask you to help them to develop good study habits, be organized, disciplined and stay focused on what's important so they can get good grades and graduate on time. God I ask that You would protect them at all times and meet their every need. Father most of all, I pray that they would have a heart to serve You.

In Jesus Name! Amen.

SCRIPTURE REFERENCE:

Romans 15:1 Amplified Bible (AMP)
15 Now we who are strong [in our convictions and faith] ought to [patiently] put up with the weaknesses of those who are not strong, and not just please ourselves.

ACCEPTANCE TO COLLEGE – VOCATIONAL SCHOOL

Father,

I thank for Your Word which says when my ways please You, that You will give me the desires of my heart. My heart's desire is to be accepted to attend **NAME THE INSTITUTION** for higher learning. You also said that when I seek first Your Kingdom and Your Righteousness that all things would be added unto me. So I thank You for being accepted to **NAME THE INSTITUTION** which is a good thing and I receive it.

In Jesus Name! Amen.

SCRIPTURE REFERENCE:

Matthew 6:33 Amplified Bible (AMP)

[33] But first *and* most importantly seek (aim at, strive after) His kingdom and His righteousness [His way of doing and being right—the attitude and character of God], and all these things will be given to you also.

DEBT FREE EDUCATION

Father,

I thank You for a debt free education, for my tuition paid in full. Your Word says If I live in You and Your Word lives in me, then I can ask You for anything that's according to Your will and You'll do it for me. I have asked, I believe I have received it and therefore I count it done.

In Jesus Name! Amen.

SCRIPTURE REFERENCE:

John 15:7 King James Version (KJV)
[7] If ye abide in me, and my words abide in you, ye shall ask what ye will, and it shall be done unto you.

TO OBTAIN SCHOLARSHIPS AND/OR GRANTS

Father,

I thank You and believe that You have ordered my steps and give me the desire to go to college. Therefore, You will grant me the desires of my heart. I thank You for making every crooked path straight and opening every door that I need to walk through. So I thank You for scholarships, and grants. I believe my tuition is paid in full. I thank You that I have favor with man because I have favor with You and I count it done.

In Jesus Name! Amen.

SCRIPTURE REFERENCE:

Psalm 37:23 Amplified Bible (AMP)
[23] The steps of a [good and righteous] man are directed *and* established by the LORD,
And He delights in his way [and blesses his path].

TO STOP BEING BULLIED

Father,

I thank You that I am hidden under the shadow of Your wings. I will never fear what people can do to me. I am not afraid because I put my trust in You. I thank You that You have assigned angels to watch over me, to protect me. I thank you for delivering me out of all afflictions, and torment. No weapon formed against me shall prosper. I thank you that vengeance belongs to you and you shall repay in full the wrongful debt of bullying that has been charged against me. I pray for those who persecute me, that you will give them peace in their heart [a] for [a]kings and all who are in [positions of] high authority, so that we may live a peaceful and quiet life in all godliness and dignity. and mind. **REPORT THIS,**

In Jesus Name! Amen.

SCRIPTURE REFERENCE:

Psa. 91:1, 11 Amplified Bible (AMP)

[1] Those who live in the shelter of the Most High
   will find rest in the shadow of the Almighty.
[11] For he will order his angels to protect you wherever you go.

TO STOP BEING A BULLY

Father,

I realize and confess that I've been a bully. I ask You to forgive me and please help me to stop. Father, heal me in the places where I hurt so I won't hurt others. Now I see I've been created to do good and not evil, to help people and do them no harm. I choose to stop. I choose to love myself and love my neighbor as I love myself. I choose to be kind, caring and attentive to the needs of others. I declare today and every day that I am no longer a bully.

In Jesus Name! Amen.

SCRIPTURE REFERENCE:

Romans 12:21 Amplified Bible (AMP)
[21] Do not be overcome *and* conquered by evil, but overcome evil with good.

TO OVERCOME PEER PRESSURE

Father,

Because it is my desire to please You in all things, in Jesus Name I thank You for friends that pressure me to do good, for friends that have my best interest at heart. I thank You for the desire to be yoked together with friends who love You and put You first; friends who put their trust in you as I do. I thank You Father for the wisdom to choose the right people to call friend, the right places to go, how long to stay and the courage to say no when I need to say no. I thank You for the strength to be who You would have me to be.

In Jesus Name!

SCRIPTURE REFERENCE:

2 Corinthians 6:14 Amplified Bible (AMP)
[14] Do not be unequally bound together with unbelievers [do not make mismatched alliances with them, inconsistent with your faith]. For what partnership can righteousness have with lawlessness? Or what fellowship can light have with darkness?

TO OVERCOME LONELINESS

Father,

I thank you for always being with me. You will never leave me or forsake me, you will be with me until the end. I thank for being that friend that stays close to me. Therefore Lord, during times that I feel lonely, I will wait on You with prayer. I will remember that you are there to comfort me, counsel me and develop me in your love, joy and peace. I now understand that it's ok to be alone but I don't ever have to feel lonely because You are always with me.

In Jesus Name!

SCRIPTURE REFERENCE:

Matthew 28:20 Amplified Bible (AMP)

[20] teaching them to observe everything that I have commanded you; and lo, I am with you always [remaining with you perpetually—regardless of circumstance, and on every occasion], even to the end of the age."

TO ABSTAIN FROM SEX

Father,

I thank you that my body does not belong to me but to You and when I honor my body I am honoring You. Therefore, by faith I choose to wait until I get married to have sex. I choose honor, I choose righteousness and I choose abstinence. I thank You for connecting me with people who choose to abstain like I do. I value me and I'm worth the wait. I thank you for the strength to separate myself from anyone who tries to entice me to do anything that dishonors You. **If anyone is encouraging you to have sex, tell your parent or a caring adult**

In Jesus Name! Amen.

SCRIPTURE REFERENCE:

1 Corinthians 6:20 Amplified Bible (AMP)
[20] You were bought with a price [you were actually purchased with the precious blood of Jesus and made His own]. So then, honor *and* glorify God with your body.

WAITING AND DATING

Father,

I confess that even though I am attracted to the opposite sex, I have made a choice to wait until I'm married to have sex. Therefore, I will not be unequally yoked with unbelievers, people who believe differently than I do. I thank you for leading me to fellowship with those who desire to obey Your Word in like manner and be an example to those who don't. I will walk with the wise, I am victorious, I am more than a conqueror and Your joy shall be my strength. I value me and I'm worth the wait.

BEST PRACTICE: HANG OUT IN GROUPS AND NOT ALONE WITH THE OPPOSITE SEX.

In Jesus Name! Amen

SCRIPTURE REFERENCE:

Proverbs 13:20 Amplified Bible (AMP)
[20] He who walks [as a companion] with wise men will be wise, But the companions of [conceited, dull-witted] fools [are fools themselves and] will experience harm.

OVERCOMING TEMPTATION

Father,

I thank You that when temptation of any kind comes, You have already prepared the way of escape for me. For I believe You would not allow me to be faced with something that would overtake me or make me stumble. Because I am in You, You will not allow me to be tempted by anything that I can't overcome. I will guard my heart and do all I can to avoid people, places and things that may open the door to temptation of any kind. Father I thank You for the victory over

_____ and all temptation.

In Jesus Name! Amen.

SCRIPTURE REFERENCE:

1 Corinthians 10:13 Easy-to-Read Version (ERV)
[13] The only temptations that you have are the same temptations that all people have. But you can trust God. He will not let you be tempted more than you can bear. But when you are tempted, God will also give you a way to escape that temptation. Then you will be able to endure it.

OVERCOMING ADDICTION

Father,

I ask You to forgive me for indulging in activities and behaviors that have been harmful to my body, relationships, my life and caused me to be disobedient to You, resulting in neglect of my priorities. Therefore, I say I am done with: social media, video games, drugs, drinking, cigarettes, blunts, vaping, weed/ marijuana, pornography, over eating, overspending, stealing, lying, and anything else that is not like You. (**SPEAK THE ADDICTION(S) that are specific to you, keep praying this way until you're built up in faith to quit!**)

In Jesus Name! Amen

SCRIPTURE REFERENCE

Philippians 4:13 King James Version (KJV)
I can do all things through Christ which strengthens me.

DELIVERANCE FROM BAD HABITS

Father,

I thank You for loving me unconditionally and setting me free to serve you. Therefore, I proclaim that I will no longer be bound by anything that is not from You. I thank You that as I call on Your name You deliver me out of it. I will no longer be enslaved, held captive or afflicted by any person, place or thing: namely

_____, I see myself free.

In Jesus Name! Amen.

SCRIPTURE REFERENCE:

John 8:36 Amplified Bible (AMP)
[36] So if the Son makes you free, then you are unquestionably free.

GOOD HEALTH

Father,

I thank you for divine health and healing in my body. I thank you that by Your stripes I am healed. Lord I thank You for a mindset to eat right and exercise as much as I possibly can and to get my proper rest so I can be and stay healthy. Jesus, I thank You for dying for me so I can be free from sickness and disease.

In Jesus Name! Amen.

SCRIPTURE REFERENCE:

1 Peter 2:24 Amplified Bible (AMP)
[24] He personally carried our sins in His body on the cross [willingly offering Himself on it, as on an altar of sacrifice], so that we might die to sin [becoming immune from the penalty and power of sin] and live for righteousness; for by His wounds you [who believe] have been healed.

HEALING FROM SICKNESS

Father,

I thank You For Jesus dying on the cross for me. I don't have to bear sickness in my body because You bore it in Yours. I am now dead to sin, sickness and disease and will live to do what is right. By His stripes I am made whole.

In Jesus Name! Amen.

SCRIPTURE REFERENCE:

I Peter 2:24 King James Version (KJV)
[24] Who his own self bare our sins in his own body on the tree, that we, being dead to sins, should live unto righteousness: by whose stripes ye were healed.

HELP IN TIME OF TROUBLE

Father,

I thank You for being my help in time of trouble. I thank You for meeting my every need. Thank You for always making a way when there seems to be no way. I thank You for opening doors that could not be opened and for closing doors that could not be closed. Lord, I thank You for fighting every battle and giving me the victory; You always cause me to win. I thank You for always protecting me and shielding me from all hurt, harm, danger, injury and accident.

In Jesus Name! Amen.

SCRIPTURE REFERENCE:

Ephesians 6:12 Amplified Bible (AMP)

[12] For our struggle is not against flesh and blood [contending only with physical opponents], but against the rulers, against the powers, against the world forces of this [present] darkness, against the spiritual *forces* of wickedness in the heavenly (supernatural) *places*.

SAFETY

Father,

I thank you for keeping me safe at all times for you have given your angels instructions to watch over me. I thank you that I am not afraid of people and what they may try to do to me because I put my trust is in you. Thank you for always keeping me safe, for hiding me under the shadow of Your wings and being my strength and protector, my present help in the time of trouble.

In Jesus Name! Amen.

SCRIPTURE REFERENCE:

Psalm 56:11 Amplified Bible (AMP)
[11] In God have I put my trust *and* confident reliance; I will not be afraid.
What can man do to me?

OVERCOMING FEAR

Father,

I thank you that because I am in You and You are in me, I don't have to be afraid of anything. Being fearful, timid or shy does not come from you. In You I have confidence, love for myself and others, self-discipline and fearless thinking so I am able to meet and exceed any challenge that comes my way. I can do all things in Your strength.

In Jesus Name! Amen.

SCRIPTURE REFERENCE:

2 Timothy 1:7 Amplified Bible (AMP)
[7] For God did not give us a spirit of timidity *or* cowardice *or* fear, but [He has given us a spirit] of power and of love and of sound judgment *and* personal discipline [abilities that result in a calm, well-balanced mind and self-control].

TO OVERCOME WORRY AND ANXIETY

Father,

I thank You for loving me, being concerned about me, and caring about the things that try to bother me from time to time. Father, I give all my worries and anxiety to You. I trust You for the wisdom to have an answer for things that need answers, by faith I believe all my needs are met. I thank You for loving me that much. I refuse to be filled with worry because I know You care about me.

In Jesus Name! Amen.

SCRIPTURE REFERENCE:

Philippians 4:6 Amplified Bible (AMP)
[6] Do not be anxious *or* worried about anything, but in everything [every circumstance and situation] by prayer and petition with thanksgiving, continue to make your [specific] requests known to God.

TO HAVE EVERYTHING I NEED

Father,

I thank you for supplying all my needs. I thank you for more than enough food, clothes, money, and transportation. I thank you that there is no lack in the kingdom, therefore, I don't have to be in lack either. I thank You for the wisdom on what I can do to earn my own money. I thank you that I am blessed coming in and going out; from the top of my head to the soles of my feet. I thank you that every good thing I put my hands to do shall prosper and have a good outcome. I thank You that All my needs are met.

In Jesus Name! Amen.

SCRIPTURE REFERENCE:

Philippians 4:19 King James Version (KJV)
[19] But my God shall supply all your need according to his riches in glory by Christ Jesus.

FAVOR

Father,

I thank You, for like Mary, I am Your good and faithful servant, I am highly favored (given special honor, benefits). The more I learn about you the more favored I am by God and people. Your goodness and mercy follows me everywhere. People are looking for me to do me good. I thank You for the doors that were once closed are now open, for You have honored and blessed me this way. I will praise you forever.

In Jesus Name.

SCRIPTURE REFERENCE:

Luke 2:52 Amplified Bible (AMP)
[52] And Jesus kept increasing in wisdom and in stature, and in favor with God and men.

TO GET A JOB

Father,

I thank You for the desire to be self-sufficient, depending on You and not people, to meet my needs. I thank You for a good paying job. I thank You that employers are looking for me and I am looking for them. I will be on time, proficient at every task, a team player and an asset to the company. I thank You for favor, for an open door of opportunity. I thank You for my new job.

In Jesus Name! Amen.

SCRIPTURE REFERENCE:

2 Corinthians 3:5 Amplified Bible (AMP)
[5] Not that we are sufficiently qualified in ourselves to claim anything as *coming* from us, but our sufficiency *and* qualifications come from God.

PROMOTION

Father,

I have the desire to advance at _____.
Your word says that as I am faithful over a little, you'll make me ruler over much and Lord I've been faithful. Therefore, I thank you for a promotion; increased pay and more responsibility. I thank You for granting the desire of my heart.

In Jesus name! Amen.

SCRIPTURE REFERENCE:

Matthew 25:21 Amplified Bible (AMP)
[21] His master said to him, 'Well done, good and faithful servant. You have been faithful *and* trustworthy over a little, I will put you in charge of many things; share in the joy of your master.'

TO WALK BY FAITH

Father,

Your Word says that faith comes by hearing. I thank You that as I pray and speak Your Word, I'm hearing Your Word and growing in faith and increasing in my walk of faith. I esteem and value Your Word above the things that I see. I will believe and obey Your Word and not my feelings. I will walk by faith and not by sight. Thank You for performing the Words that I speak.

In Jesus Name! Amen.

SCRIPTURE REFERENCE

Mark 11:23-24 Amplified Bible, Classic (AMPC)

[23] Truly I tell you, whoever says to this mountain, Be lifted up and thrown into the sea! and does not doubt at all in his heart but believes that what he says will take place, it will be done for him.

[24] For this reason I am telling you, whatever you ask for in prayer, believe (trust and be confident) that it is granted to you, and you will [get it].

TO FORGIVE MYSELF

Father,

I ask you to forgive me for _____ You said that if I confess my sin, that you are faithful and just to forgive me. Not only do You forgive me but You also cleanse me of all unrighteousness. Therefore, I thank you that my sin has been removed from me and now I stand before you pure, holy and blessed. I thank you that I am forgiven and I forgive myself.

In Jesus Name! Amen.

SCRIPTURE REFERENCE:

1 John 1:9 Amplified Bible (AMP)
[9] If we [freely] admit that we have sinned *and* confess our sins, He is faithful and just [true to His own nature and promises], and will forgive our sins and cleanse us *continually* from all unrighteousness [our wrongdoing, everything not in conformity with His will and purpose].

TO FORGIVE OTHERS

Father,

Because I desire to always be right with you, I choose to forgive. I realize that forgiveness is a choice and not a feeling. Feelings of anger and resentment may be present but I will remind myself that I have chosen to forgive. I forgive them because you have forgiven me of everything I've ever done or ever will do. You don't hold anything against me. Therefore, I will not hold a grudge against

_____either.

In Jesus Name! Amen.

SCRIPTURE REFFERENCE:

Matthew 18:21-23 Amplified Bible (AMP)

[21] Then Peter came to Him and asked, "Lord, how many times will my brother sin against me and I forgive him *and* let it go? Up to seven times?"

[22] Jesus answered him, "I say to you, not up to seven times, but seventy times seven.

TO WALK IN LOVE

Father,

Because You love me unconditionally, I have been adopted into Your family and the same love You have for me, I choose to have for myself. I'm grateful that Your love for me is based on who I am and not what I do. Therefore, I will love my neighbor as I love myself, without pre-conditions, regardless of race, gender or socio-economic status. My faith will not work without love, it is the more excellent way to live, to walk in love.

In Jesus Name! Amen.

SCRIPTURE REFERENCE:

1 Corinthians 13:4-8 New International Version (NIV) [4] Love is patient, love is kind. It does not envy, it does not boast, it is not proud. [5] It does not dishonor others, it is not self-seeking, it is not easily angered, it keeps no record of wrongs. [6] Love does not delight in evil but rejoices with the truth. [7] It always protects, always trusts, always hopes, always perseveres. [8] Love never fails. But where there are prophecies, they will cease; where there are tongues, they will be stilled: where there is knowledge, it will pass away.

TO EXERCISE PATIENCE

Father,

I thank you for helping me to exercise patience. It's already ingrained in my spirit so when trouble comes patience is at work to help me rejoice through it. When my faith is being tested, my patience will go to work reminding me that I win. When I feel weak, patience will come and give me strength and hope and help me to endure. When I need a miracle, a blessing, patience will keep me in peace until it comes. Thank You Lord for your patience.

In Jesus Name! Amen.

SCRIPTURE REFERENCE:

James 1:3-4 Amplified Bible (AMP)

[3] Be assured that the testing of your faith [through experience] produces endurance [leading to spiritual maturity, and inner peace]. [4] And let endurance have its perfect result *and* do a thorough work, so that you may be perfect and completely developed [in your faith], lacking in nothing.

TO HAVE INNER PEACE

Father,

I thank You that Jesus left me the gift of Peace, the Peace that keeps me, the Peace that leads me, the Peace that will even fight for me. Lord I thank You that Peace keeps me calm, well balanced and self-controlled. So I will keep thinking about You and keep my peace. I won't worry anymore because I know you hear my prayers. I will stay calm God because I trust You.

In Jesus Name! Amen.

SCRIPTURE REFERENCE

Philippians 4:6-7 Living Bible (TLB)

[6] Don't worry about anything; instead, pray about everything; tell God your needs, and don't forget to thank him for his answers. [7] If you do this, you will experience God's peace, which is far more wonderful than the human mind can understand. His peace will keep your thoughts and your hearts quiet and at rest as you trust in Christ Jesus.

TO HAVE A GOOD ATTITUDE - TO BE HUMBLE

Father,

I repent and ask you to forgive me for having a bad attitude. I will think highly of myself but not more than highly than I should and bring glory to Your name. I choose to humble myself and respect my Elders and my peers. Father, I thank you for the grace to do what's right in Your sight. I thank You that as I humble myself You won't have to humble me but You will lift me up when the time is right.

In Jesus Name! Amen

SCRIPTURE REFERENCE

Romans 12:3 Amplified Bible (AMP)
[3] For by the grace [of God] given to me I say to every one of you not to think more highly of himself [and of his importance and ability] than he ought to think; but to think so as to have sound judgment, as God has apportioned to each a degree of faith [and a purpose designed for service].

TO OVERCOME DEPRESSION – FEELING SAD

Father,

I thank You for hearing me when I call. When I praise You, I'm lifted out of sadness and depression and my mood changes. When I speak Your word, my thoughts turn toward you and I remember Your goodness and mercy toward me and that all things are working for my good. Father, I choose to trade depression and sadness for peace and joy. I trade the spirit of heaviness for the garment of praise and I am helped. I choose to remember things that are good, true, lovely, virtuous, praise worthy and just. **PRAISE HIM NOW!**

In Jesus Name! Amen

SCRIPTURE REFERENCE:

Philippians 4:8 New Living Translation (NLT)

[8] And now, dear brothers and sisters, one final thing. Fix your thoughts on what is true, and honorable, and right, and pure, and lovely, and admirable. Think about things that are excellent and worthy of praise.

TO OVERCOME THOUGHTS OF SUICIDE

Father,

I believe You want me to live, I choose to believe that no matter what mistakes I make, You always forgive me, reminding me that I win. Whatever difficulties I face, the lies the devil tells me about myself and others or the depression I feel; I will daily choose to live the life You have ordained for me. Suicide is permanent, my situation is temporary and will be over soon. I will let Your love sustain me, give me hope and strength. I will think on things that are good, praise worthy, true and virtuous. I choose to live. **ARE THINKING ABOUT SUICIDE? TALK TO A PARENT OR CARUNG ADULT.**

In Jesus Name! Amen.

SCRIPTURE REFERENCE:
Philippians 4:8 King James Version (KJV).
[8] Finally, brethren, whatsoever things are true, whatsoever things are honest, whatsoever things are just, whatsoever things are pure, whatsoever things are lovely, whatsoever things are of good report; if there be any virtue, and if there be any praise, think on these things.

TO BE SECURE IN MY BORN GENDER

Father,

I thank You for creating me. You didn't make a mistake or change Your mind about anything concerning me after I was born. Even though my feelings tell me I'm attracted to the same sex or that I'm trapped in the wrong body, that's a lie and I refuse to accept it. **I WILL NOT** accept or choose what has chosen me. I will not give in to confusion. I will live by faith and not my feelings or thoughts that are contrary to Your perfect plan for me.

(If you have or are currently participating in a contrary lifestyle, ask God to forgive you and pray the prayer of **OVERCOME ADDICTION).**

In Jesus Name! Amen.

SCRIPTURE RFERENCE:

II Corinthians 10:5 English Standard Version (ESV)

We destroy arguments and every lofty opinion raised against the knowledge of God, and take every thought captive to obey Christ.

TO ACCEPT CHRIST

Father,

I confess that I am a sinner and I need a savior. I ask you to forgive me of my sins, to come into my heart and be my Lord and Savior. I say with my mouth and believe in my heart that you sent Your Son Jesus to die for me and on the third day You rose from the dead that I might be free from sin. I invite You to come into my heart and be my Lord. I thank You Lord that now I'm saved! **TELL SOMEONE THAT YOU HAVE ACCEPTED CHRIST.**

In Jesus Name, I'm saved! Amen.

SCRIPTURE REFERENCE

Romans 10:8-10 King James Version (KJV)
[8] But what saith it? The word is nigh thee, even in thy mouth, and in thy heart: that is, the word of faith, which we preach;[9] That if thou shalt confess with thy mouth the Lord Jesus, and shalt believe in thine heart that God hath raised him from the dead, thou shalt be saved. [10] For with the heart man believeth unto righteousness; and with the mouth confession is made unto salvation.

RECEIVE THE BAPTISM OF THE HOLY SPIRIT

Father,

Because I am saved, I ask You to fill me now with the Holy Spirit with the evidence of speaking in other tongues. You said when I ask for the Holy Spirit you will give it to me and I will receive power to serve You and tell more people about You. You said all I need to do is ask and I shall receive. So, Father, I ask You now and thank You. I speak in tongues now! **By faith, raise your hands, open your mouth and start speaking.**

In Jesus Name! Amen.

SCRIPTURE REFERENCES

Luke 11:10-13 New Century Version (NCV)
[10] Yes, everyone who asks will receive. The one who searches will find. And everyone who knocks will have the door opened. [11] If your children ask for[a] a fish, which of you would give them a snake instead? [12] Or, if your children ask for an egg, would you give them a scorpion? [13] Even though you are bad, you know how to give good things to your children. How much more your heavenly Father will give the Holy Spirit to those who ask him!"

BE A WITNESS FOR CHRIST

Father,

I thank You for the courage to win souls. Your Word says that this is what wise people do. Jesus, You died for everyone because You want all men to be saved. I thank You Lord for the power to be a witness everywhere I go, to tell people about your love, and all your many benefits by faith. I will pray the Prayer of Salvation with many people.

In Jesus Name! Amen.

SCRIPTURE REFERENCE

Acts 1:8 Amplified Bible (AMP)
[8] But you will receive power *and* ability when the Holy Spirit comes upon you; and you will be My witnesses [to tell people about Me] both in Jerusalem and in all Judea, and Samaria, and even to the ends of the earth."

Author Biography:

Ms. Toy has a passion for young adults which is the reason for this book, to help you in your journey toward greatness. Her prayer writing journey began 40 years ago as a prayer reading journey. As a young Christian, who didn't grow up in church, she quickly realized the need for prayer and also realized that she didn't know how to pray. So she bought a prayer book and daily prayed every prayer in that book as well as others. Never knowing that she was sowing seeds that would one day reap a harvest. That harvest being helping others in prayer the same way she was helped, with a prayer book.

Prayer must to be according to God's Word if it's going to be effective. You can rest assured that every prayer in this book is based on God's Word and they will be answered. So pray every day and get ready to receive what you are believing for.

More **I CAN HAVE WHAT I SAY** prayer books:

My Healing Scriptures and Confessions

Everyday Prayers for Teens

Everyday Prayers for Adults

The Struggle Was Real …Until I Said It Was Over

For order information and to see our other products go to: **icanhavewhatisay.com** Feel free to email your prayer request or leave us a review to: **icanhavewhatisay@gmail.com**

I'm Praying for You! Sincerely Ms. Toy

www.ingramcontent.com/pod-product-compliance
Lightning Source LLC
Chambersburg PA
CBHW071140280326
41935CB00010B/1304